Dear Parent:
Your child's love of reading starts here!

Every child learns to read in a different way and at his or her own speed. Some go back and forth between reading levels and read favorite books again and again. Others read through each level in order. You can help your young reader improve and become more confident by encouraging his or her own interests and abilities. From books your child reads with you to the first books he or she reads alone, there are I Can Read Books for every stage of reading:

SHARED READING
Basic language, word repetition, and whimsical illustrations, ideal for sharing with your emergent reader

BEGINNING READING
Short sentences, familiar words, and simple concepts for children eager to read on their own

READING WITH HELP
Engaging stories, longer sentences, and language play for developing readers

READING ALONE
Complex plots, challenging vocabulary, and high-interest topics for the independent reader

ADVANCED READING
Short paragraphs, chapters, and exciting themes
for the perfect bridge to chapter books

I Can Read Books have introduced children to the joy of reading since 1957. Featuring award-winning authors and illustrators and a fabulous cast of beloved characters, I Can Read Books set the standard for beginning readers.

A lifetime of discovery begins with the magical words **"I Can Read!"**

Visit www.icanread.com for information
on enriching your child's reading experience.

To Emma
—D.G.

To John Lynch, art teacher and friend
—J.P.

*The author gratefully acknowledges the editorial
contributions of Lori Houran.*

I Can Read Book® is a trademark of HarperCollins Publishers.

My Weird School Goes to the Museum. Text copyright © 2016 by Dan Gutman. Illustrations copyright © 2016 by Jim Paillot. All rights reserved. Printed in the United States of America. No part of this book may be used or reproduced in any manner whatsoever without written permission except in the case of brief quotations embodied in critical articles and reviews. For information address HarperCollins Children's Books, a division of HarperCollins Publishers, 195 Broadway, New York, NY 10007   www.icanread.com

Library of Congress Control Number: 2016931800
ISBN 978-0-06-236742-6 (pbk. bdg.)—ISBN 978-0-06-236744-0 (hardcover)

16 17 18 19 20   WOR   10 9 8 7 6 5 4 3 2   ❖   First Edition

I Can Read!

READING
2
WITH HELP

My WeiRd School

Goes to the Museum

Dan Gutman

Pictures by **Jim Paillot**

HARPER

An Imprint of HarperCollinsPublishers

My name is Andrea

and I LOVE school!

I love tests! I love homework!

I love teachers—

and teachers love ME!

"Teacher's pet!" A.J. calls me.
He thinks it's an insult,
but I love it.
Who *wouldn't* want to be
the teacher's favorite?

A.J., that's who.

All he wants to be is class clown.

He doesn't even care

that he's in gifted and talented.

I LOVE being in gifted and talented!

We're the only ones in the class.

So we get to go on field trips,

just the two of us.

"Ooooh," Ryan said this morning.

"A.J. and Andrea are going

to the art museum together.

They must be in *love*!"

Well, duh. Of course we are.

A.J. just doesn't know it yet.

"When are you two getting married?"

said Michael.

"NEVER!" yelled A.J.

Ha. That's what he thinks.

"Remember to *behave* at the museum,"
warned Mr. Cooper.
He looked at A.J. when he said it.
Teachers never look at me
when they give warnings.

A.J. and I took our own tiny bus

to the art museum.

A man met us outside.

He was really old,

with hair growing out of his ears.

"I'm the museum educator," he said.

Ooooh, an educator!

In other words, a *teacher*.

He was going to love me!

The man led us inside . . . very slowly.

"Excuse me, sir," I said.

He didn't hear me.

"EXCUSE ME, SIR," I said louder.

"WHAT'S YOUR NAME?"

"Mr. Meezer," he answered.

"More like Mr. *Geezer*," said A.J.

He started giggling.

"Shhh!" I told him. "Cut it out!"

Mr. Meezer turned around.

I thought he was going

to frown at A.J.

But he frowned at me!

Mr. Meezer shuffled ahead.

"This painting was just donated to the museum," he said.

"Good thing they didn't pay for it," said A.J. "It's just a bunch of dumb circles!"

I sighed.

"It's NOT just circles. It must mean something very deep and important. What's it called?"

A.J. read the sign next to it.

"*Just Circles*," he said. "HA!"

It got worse when A.J. saw a statue.

"It's naked!" he said.

"No, it's *nude*," I corrected him.

"What's the difference?" said A.J.

"I can still see its butt!"

I was getting really annoyed.

"Arlo Jervis," I said.

I like to call A.J. by his real name,

especially when I'm mad.

It's good practice

for when we're married.

"We're looking at fine art,

and all you see is a BUTT?"

I didn't mean to,

but I said "butt" really loud.

It echoed through the museum.

Mr. Meezer gasped.

"Young lady! Stop saying that.
You're acting very immature!"

WHAT?!

"But—but—" I said.

"I TOLD you to stop saying that!"
said Mr. Meezer.

A.J. laughed so hard he fell down.

"Mr. Cooper said one of you
might misbehave,"
Mr. Meezer muttered.
"Now I know who he meant."

This was HORRIBLE!

How could Mr. Meezer think

I was the troublemaker?

From now on, I had to be *perfect*.

We went to the next room.

It was full of swords and shields.

Tall suits of armor stood in a row.

"Cool!" said A.J.

"Look, but don't touch,"

warned Mr. Meezer.

He looked at me when he said it.

At ME!

I took a deep breath

to calm myself down.

I felt something tickle my nose.

That armor was awfully dusty. . . .

"Ah—ah—ah—" I said. "Ah-CHOO!"

My sneeze knocked me off-balance.

I bumped into a suit of armor.

CLANG! It fell down.

CLANG! It knocked over

the next suit of armor.

CLANG! CLANG! CLANG! CLANG!
CLANG! CLANG! CLANG! CLANG!
All the armor crashed to the floor!

"I'm so sorry, Mr. Geezer!" I cried.

"I mean, Mr. *Meezer*!"

"That's it!" he snapped.

"I'm sending you back to school—

with a note to your teacher!"

Noooooooooooooooooooooooooo!

A.J. tried to talk to me
on the bus back to school.
"Look on the bright side, Andrea.
Now that Mr. Cooper will hate you,
I'll stop calling you teacher's pet!"
"I LOVE being called that,
you dumbhead!" I shouted.

At school, I went straight to Mr. Cooper.

I unfolded the note.

"*Dear Mr. Cooper,*" I read out loud.

"*One of your students misbehaved*
at the museum today."

I gulped. This was it.

I started to read my name.

"*And*—"

"*And* it was ME, of course!"

yelled A.J.

He ripped the note out of my hands
and crumpled it up.

"Oh, A.J." Mr. Cooper sighed.

"I'm disappointed in you."

"Oh, A.J." I sighed. "I love you!

And now I'm sure you love me too!"

I didn't say it out loud, of course.

But it was true.

Why else would he save me like that?

A.J. was my knight in shining armor!

Will A.J. ever admit he loves me?

Will I always be Mr. Cooper's pet?

Will I go back to the museum

and follow Mr. Meezer for days

until he makes me his teacher's pet too?

OF COURSE!

It will be easy!